HOW ARE THEY **DIFFERENT?**

Tell Me the DIFFERENCE Between an

ALLIGATOR
and a CROCODILE

Leigh Rockwood

PowerKiDS
press.

New York

5/13

Published in 2013 by The Rosen Publishing Group, Inc.
29 East 21st Street, New York, NY 10010

Copyright © 2013 by The Rosen Publishing Group, Inc.

All rights reserved. No part of this book may be reproduced in any form without permission in writing from the publisher, except by a reviewer.

First Edition

Editor: Joanne Randolph
Book Design: Kate Laczynski

Photo Credits: Cover (alligator) Don Johnston/All Canada Photos/Getty Images; cover (crocodile) Gert Johannes Jacobus Vrey/Shutterstock.com; pp. 4, 8 iStockphoto/Thinkstock; p. 5 Eric Gevaert/Shutterstock.com; p. 6 Eric Gevaert/Shutterstock.com; p. 7 (left) Tier Und Naturfotografie J. und C. Sohns/Photographer's Choice/Getty Images; p. 7 (right) Peter Walton Photography/Photolibrary/Getty Images; p. 9 Hemera/Thinkstock; p. 10 Stephen St. John/National Geographic Image Collection/Getty Images; p. 11 David Tipling/The Image Bank/Getty Images; p. 12 © iStockphoto.com/studioraffi; p. 13 © iStockphoto.com/mongkol chakritthakool; p. 14 SunnyS/Shutterstock.com; p. 15 Gerrit_de_Vries/Shutterstock.com; p. 16 Ohmega1982/Shutterstock.com; p. 17 Delmas Lehman/Shutterstock.com; p. 19 Brian Lasenby/Shutterstock.com; p. 20 Bob Elsdale/The Image Bank/Getty Images; p. 21 Ed Reschke/Peter Arnold/Getty Images; p. 22 Wayne Lynch/All Canada Photos/Getty Images.

Library of Congress Cataloging-in-Publication Data

Rockwood, Leigh.
 Tell me the difference between an alligator and a crocodile / by Leigh Rockwood. — 1st ed.
   p. cm. — (How are they different?)
Includes index.
ISBN 978-1-4488-9635-6 (library binding) — ISBN 978-1-4488-9728-5 (pbk.) —
ISBN 978-1-4488-9729-2 (6-pack)
1. Alligators—Juvenile literature. 2. Crocodiles—Juvenile literature. I. Title.
QL666.C925R644 2013
597.98'4—dc23

                          2012019322

Manufactured in the United States of America

CPSIA Compliance Information: Batch #W13PK5: For Further Information contact Rosen Publishing, New York, New York at 1-800-237-9932

CONTENTS

WHAT'S A CROCODILIAN?

Alligators and crocodiles are **reptiles** that belong to an order, or grouping, of animals called Crocodylia. The 23 **species** in this order are called crocodilians. Alligators, crocodiles, caimans, and gharials are all crocodilians.

Crocodilians, such as these crocodiles, have scaly hides and powerful jaws.

From a distance, it can be hard to tell alligators, such as this one, and crocodiles, such as those in the facing image, apart.

Because they are related, crocodilians have many things in common with one another. For example, crocodilians have been around for over 200 million years. That means that they existed at the same time as many dinosaurs! This book will focus on alligators and crocodiles, which are the best-known crocodilians. You will learn more about these reptiles, including how to tell the difference between an alligator and a crocodile.

ALL IN THE FAMILIES

Scientists classify alligators and crocodiles into two scientific families. The Alligatoridae family includes the two species of alligators and the six species of caimans. The Crocodylidae family includes the 14 species of crocodiles and the false gharial.

Alligators live in the southern United States and in eastern China. Crocodiles are found in

Caimans are generally smaller than alligators and crocodiles and have narrower snouts.

Saltwater crocodiles are the largest species of crocodilian, growing up to 23 feet (7 m) long. They live in fresh, brackish, and salty waters from eastern India and Southeast Asia to northern Australia.

American alligators live in freshwater rivers, lakes, and swamps in the southeastern United States. The largest American populations are in Florida and Louisiana.

North America, Central America, South America, Australia, Asia, and Africa. If you were in a boat on the Nile River, in Africa, you could be sure that any crocodilian you saw would be a crocodile. If you were in southern Florida, you would need to know more about the animal to identify it as an alligator or a crocodile.

HOW ARE ALLIGATORS AND CROCODILES ALIKE?

Crocodilians that are on land sometimes use a belly crawl to move, as lizards do. Unlike most lizards, they can also lift their bellies off the ground to walk, though. This is called a high walk.

The reason alligators and crocodiles can be hard to tell apart is because they have many things in common. Both animals have bodies suited to a **semiaquatic** life. They have their eyes set on top of their heads as well as nostrils set on top of their snouts. This means they can breathe and look for **prey** when the rest of their bodies are underwater.

Both alligators and crocodiles have four partly webbed toes on each back foot. These help them swim as fast as 20 miles per hour (32 km/h). Both also have five separated toes on each front foot. These help alligators and crocodiles climb onto land and dig holes in which they can rest.

Partially webbed feet help alligators and crocodiles swim. They also both have binocular vision, which helps them hunt.

CHECK OUT THE SNOUT!

One of the first things you can do to tell an alligator from a crocodile is to check out the snout. Crocodiles generally have pointed snouts, while alligators generally have more rounded snouts.

The alligator's jaw is stronger than the crocodile's and can crunch through things like turtle shells.

Can you see how these crocodiles' snouts almost come to a point? That is very different from how alligators' snouts (right) look. Do you see the U shape of the alligator's snout?

Crocodilians are one of the few reptiles that have special parts inside their mouths that let them breathe even when their mouths are full of water. This part also lets them bite animals underwater without getting water in their lungs.

You can also identify a crocodilian by looking at its closed mouth. You can see only the top teeth when an alligator's mouth is closed. That is because an alligator's upper jaw is a little bit bigger than its lower jaw, so the bottom teeth are hidden when its mouth is closed.

COMPARING ALLIGATORS

SNOUT	U-shaped
ACTIVE DURING THE DAY OR NIGHT	Night
SCIENTIFIC FAMILY	Alligatoridae
LIFE SPAN	30–60 years
DIET	Carnivore
LEGS	No fringe on hind legs
FEET	Webbed hind feet
COLOR	Blackish or grayish

and CROCODILES

V-shaped	**SNOUT**
Night	**ACTIVE DURING THE DAY OR NIGHT**
Crocodylidae	**SCIENTIFIC FAMILY**
50–75 years	**LIFE SPAN**
Carnivore	**DIET**
Fringe on hind legs	**LEGS**
Webbed hind feet	**FEET**
Olive green or brown	**COLOR**

LET'S TALK ABOUT TEETH!

Alligators have a large tooth in their lower jaws that slips into a socket, or hole, in the upper jaws when they close their mouths. In crocodiles, this big tooth as well as the rest of their upper and lower teeth are easily visible when their mouths are closed. The crocodilian's

An alligator's top teeth can be seen with its mouth closed, but its bottom teeth cannot.

14

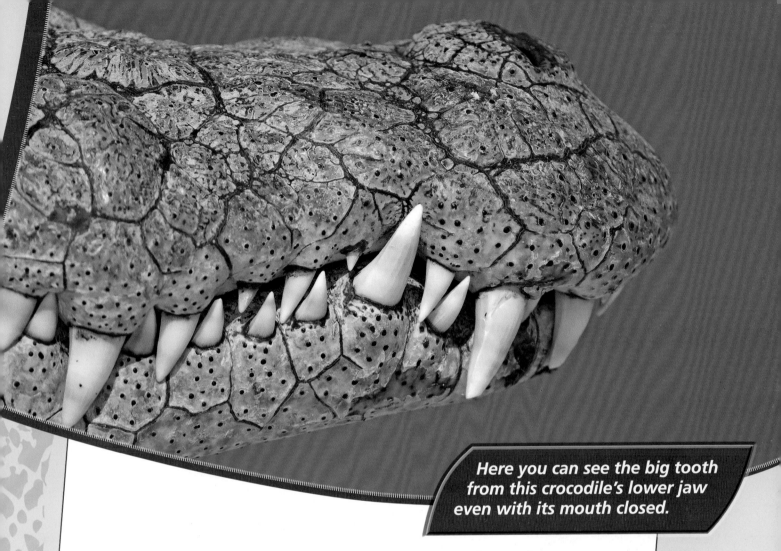

Here you can see the big tooth from this crocodile's lower jaw even with its mouth closed.

teeth are made for killing prey, rather than chewing. Both alligators and crocodiles either swallow their food whole or tear off big pieces to swallow.

Alligators and crocodiles are carnivores, which means they eat other animals for food. They eat fish, turtles, mammals, and pretty much anything that comes close enough for them to snap up!

LOOK AT THOSE LEGS

Another place to look for differences between alligators and crocodiles is on their legs. Crocodiles have fringes on the backs of their hind legs, but alligators do not.

Here you can see the partial webbing on this crocodile's hind foot.

Alligators and crocodiles can move quickly through the water, but much of the time they lie still. They look a lot like logs floating in the water, which helps them blend in and surprise prey.

On land, both kinds of crocodilians can run short distances at up to 10 miles per hour (16 km/h). They are better suited to moving in the water, though. There, they can move twice as fast as they do on land. Most of the time they are in the water, alligators and crocodiles float like logs, with their legs tucked up against their bodies.

Alligators and crocodiles live mostly in different parts of the world. They also live in different **habitats** within their ranges. Alligators stick mostly to freshwater lakes, swamps, and slow-moving rivers. Crocodiles live in these kinds of habitats, too, but they also can live in **brackish**, or somewhat salty waters, called mangrove swamps.

Crocodiles can live in saltier water because they have special **glands** on their tongues that help them get rid of excess salt in their bodies. Although alligators also have this gland, theirs does not work as well as the crocodile's, so they do their best to stick to freshwater habitats.

This American alligator lies on the banks of a bayou, or swamp, in Louisiana. Its coloring helps it blend in with its surroundings. This is called camouflage.

BABY CROCODILIANS

Alligators and crocodiles are very much alike when it comes to **mating** and having babies. If they have reached an adult size, females that are 10 to 12 years old and males that are about 16 years old are ready for mating.

Here a mother crocodile guards her clutch of eggs. Some crocodilian species carry their babies inside their mouths once they hatch. Not many predators would dare to take a baby from there!

After mating, the female prepares a nest on land where she will lay between 35 and 50 eggs. The mother guards her eggs until they **hatch**. She may even help her hatchlings hatch by biting open the leathery shells.

Crocodilian hatchlings stay with their mother for one to two years, depending on the species. Even so, only about 20 percent of the hatchlings will live to see adulthood.

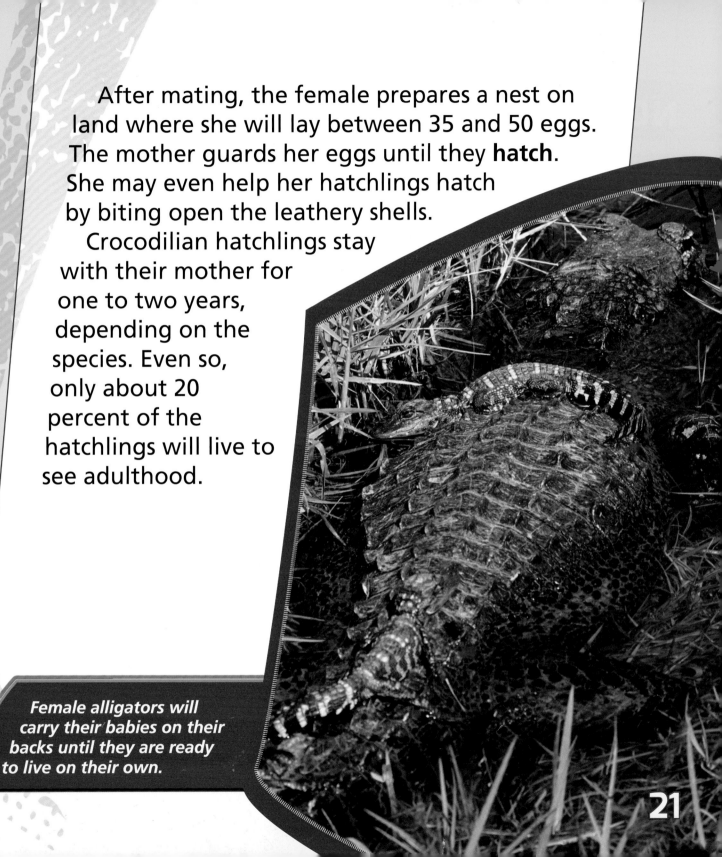

Female alligators will carry their babies on their backs until they are ready to live on their own.

The next time you visit a zoo, you will know how to tell the difference between alligators and crocodiles. Sadly, many crocodilian species are in trouble. American alligators have bounced back from being **endangered**. Chinese

Not too long ago, American alligators, such as this one, were in trouble. Thanks to lots of hard work by conservation groups, American alligators are doing better than ever before.

alligators and four crocodile species are **critically endangered**, though, and three crocodile species are listed as **vulnerable**. Groups like Defenders of Wildlife work to encourage governments to enforce laws to protect crocodilians so that these ancient animals can continue to live on Earth.

GLOSSARY

brackish (BRA-kish) Somewhat salty.

critically endangered (KRIH-tih-kuh-lee in-DAYN-jerd) In great danger of becoming extinct.

endangered (in-DAYN-jerd) In danger of no longer living.

glands (GLANDZ) Body parts that make matter to help the body do certain jobs.

habitats (HA-buh-tats) The surroundings where animals or plants naturally live.

hatch (HACH) To come out of an egg.

mating (MAYT-ing) Coming together to make babies.

prey (PRAY) An animal that is hunted by another animal for food.

reptiles (REP-tylz) Cold-blooded animals with thin, dry pieces of skin called scales.

semiaquatic (seh-mee-uh-KWAH-tik) Lives in water part of the time.

species (SPEE-sheez) One kind of living thing. All people are one species.

vulnerable (VUL-neh-ruh-bel) Open to being hurt or becoming extinct.

INDEX

WEBSITES

Due to the changing nature of Internet links, PowerKids Press has developed an online list of websites related to the subject of this book. This site is updated regularly. Please use this link to access the list: www.powerkidslinks.com/hatd/alcro/

1206321
J 597.98 Ro
$16⁹⁹